Elementals And Nature-Spirits

G. de Purucker

Kessinger Publishing's Rare Reprints

Thousands of Scarce and Hard-to-Find Books
on These and other Subjects!

- Americana
- Ancient Mysteries
- Animals
- Anthropology
- Architecture
- Arts
- Astrology
- Bibliographies
- Biographies & Memoirs
- Body, Mind & Spirit
- Business & Investing
- Children & Young Adult
- Collectibles
- Comparative Religions
- Crafts & Hobbies
- Earth Sciences
- Education
- Ephemera
- Fiction
- Folklore
- Geography
- Health & Diet
- History
- Hobbies & Leisure
- Humor
- Illustrated Books
- Language & Culture
- Law
- Life Sciences

- Literature
- Medicine & Pharmacy
- Metaphysical
- Music
- Mystery & Crime
- Mythology
- Natural History
- Outdoor & Nature
- Philosophy
- Poetry
- Political Science
- Science
- Psychiatry & Psychology
- Reference
- Religion & Spiritualism
- Rhetoric
- Sacred Books
- Science Fiction
- Science & Technology
- Self-Help
- Social Sciences
- Symbolism
- Theatre & Drama
- Theology
- Travel & Explorations
- War & Military
- Women
- Yoga
- *Plus Much More!*

We kindly invite you to view our catalog list at:
http://www.kessinger.net

ELEMENTALS AND NATURE-SPIRITS

QUESTION: "Do you think the gods ever tire of laughing at us humans?"

Do *you* think so? I think that they are laughing all the time in a quiet, silent way, very much as we humans smile at the antics of the beasts — the antics of the dog, of the sheep, at the queer movements of the worm, at the buzzing mosquito, and the fugitive fly. We laugh and ponder and wonder at this mysterious Universe of ours, in which such multitudes of animate beings exist — and all so apparently different as among themselves. We think that we understand a little about them, because they evoke in us a sense of humor and we laugh at them. Now, how about the antics that we humans play on the stage of life — you, I, all human beings: thinking our little thoughts, solving our problems — seeming to us so difficult, so profound, that at times it appears to us as if the fate of the entire Universe depended upon the solution of these problems that we strive to arrive at?

I think that the gods are laughing at us all the time; and their quiet laughter takes the form of the gentle rain and of the sunshine and of the rays from the stars and of the painted heavens at chill morn and at dewy eve; so that we sense that the gods are filled with their own silent and universal understanding of Nature's laws, which understanding is so wonderful and so majestic, because it is not disturbed by passion, because it is not fevered, because it is not hurried; it is like the silent and gentle laughter of a kindly heart, shedding its balm on us — on *us*. We human beings are full of pranks. And why shouldn't we be? I don't offer this query by way of explanation; but merely ask the question: Why shouldn't we be? Why shouldn't the dog, or the horse, or the cow, or the mosquito, or the eel, or the rat, or the rabbit, do each one its own particular work in the station of life which it has attained at the present time in its advance along the evolutionary pathway? The gods laugh at us indeed — not unkindly; but nevertheless they laugh at us in the majestic silences, much as we laugh at the antics of the beasts beneath us.

The gods understand. They have been where we now are. They were men, or beings equivalent to human beings, in some far past cosmic age: in some solar system, which is now evanished, mayhap, out of even the recollection of the gods themselves. Comprehension is understanding, and genuine understanding is always kindly. It is the heart which does not understand which judges, and judges unfairly. The French have a proverb derived from Montaigne; they say: *Tout comprendre c'est tout pardonner* —"to understand all is to forgive all." This by no means implies an approval of things which are wrong; but it does mean that with the understanding heart we can see behind the veil, behind the crust of circumstance, behind the shell of conditions, which covers the causes and reasons of things; and thus seeing with an understanding heart, we can forgive. Forgiveness, however, is something entirely different from condoning. We can forgive a fellow human-creature for his faults, for his so-called sins, for the injury that he does to us or to others. We do not condone, for condoning wrong means that one becomes *particeps criminis* — a partner in the crime, a participator in the wrong-doing; but forgiveness is divine.

The gods laugh at us because they understand us; for they have been where we now are, much as we have been little children. We forgive the little children; we forgive the little child its faults and its pranks; but we ourselves do not do as the little children do. And therefore I say in answer to this question: Yes, the gods laugh quietly at us all the time and in the immense Silence.

But how about those other vast hordes, classes, families, hosts, armies, of entities not so progressed as the gods, which fill universal Being full, and which undertake the smaller tasks in the Cosmic Work, even as mankind undertakes its own tasks: I mean those beings between us humans on the one hand and the so-called insensate atom on the other — elementals, nature-spirits, nature-sprites, gnomes, elves, kobolds, goblins, fairies — call them what you like. These names are indeed but names — names that our ancestors gave to these hosts of imperfectly developed entities. Don't be frightened at a mere name: try to get the thought, to understand the idea. Nature is full of impulses of all kinds, high and low, good and bad, peaceful and otherwise, gentle and violent, kindly and malignant. Whence do these impulses come? Where do they arise? They proceed from animate entities. Obviously an incomputable number of these impulses are imperfect; and the proof is that we see the work of imperfection all around us. It is abundantly true that we see grandeur; that we see sublimity; that we see glory; that we see relatively perfect work; we also see such accuracy in Nature's operations and structure that it astounds us; but we likewise see imperfection — what men call evil, inharmony.

Whence does all this welter of conflicting impulses come? Whence do these things that we see, arise? Yes, I ask it again: Whence? They are indeed there, and our minds are fully cognisant of their existence.

Now, the only source of disharmony, of imperfection, of evil-doing, of inability to produce perfect results, *that human beings know of,* is in human beings; yet we see these same imperfections outside of us; and too many of us say — for we cheat ourselves with words and say — that they 'just are.' Have they no cause? Of course they have; and we are cheating ourselves with words if we conclude otherwise. They have causes; and it is obvious that imperfection arises only from an imperfect source, *i. e.,* in imperfect beings. These imperfectly evolved beings have their places in the boundless scheme of things just as we humans have, just as the gods have, just as the super-gods have, and at the other end of the scale, just as the atoms have. Because these entities are imperfect, therefore their works are imperfect.

A generalizing term we may call these imperfectly evolved entities by, is 'sprites' or nature-spirits; but I like the good old Theosophical term, *Elementals,* which means beings who are beginning a course of evolutionary growth, and who therefore are in the elemental states of their growth. How did they come into our Universe? How did *we* come here? We are here; they are here. Is it not obvious that there is a cause for these things that we have spoken of? Human beings on earth — are they the only animate, quasi-intelligent, quasi-intellectual, thinking, conscious entities in boundless infinitude? Consider that the beasts, the plants, yes, and as the Theosophist says, even the minerals, are all possessed each in its own degree of life, of animation, of a certain portion of an intellectual essence: for the Cosmic Soul permeates all things as an Ocean of Life; the Cosmic Life permeates all things as the Cosmic Soul; and all things and all entities everywhere are but the children of this Cosmic Life-Consciousness; and as our earth is not the only seat or dwelling-place of sentient and animate beings — which supposition is transparently absurd — therefore consciousnesses and lives and animate beings exist in families, races, in hordes, in armies, in incomputable multitudes, everywhere.

An Elemental, my Brothers, is a being who has entered our Universe on the lowest plane or in the lowest world, or degree, or step, of that Universe, on the rising Stairway of Life, and this Stairway of Life begins in any Universe at the lowest stage of that Universe, and ends for that Universe in that Universe's highest stage — its own Cosmic Spirit. Our Universe is not the only one in infinitude. Boundless Space is filled with innumerable Universes. You cannot count them, so numerous are they. Our Universe is only one of them. Infinitude is filled with them. And these Universes interpenetrate each other, the rivers of living beings flowing from one Universe into some other Universe and backwards in the waves of life as they sweep through boundless space. Mark you, friends, when I speak of Boundless Infinitude I do not mean only this physical universe, which is but one cross-section, so to speak, of infinite Space. I mean particularly those inner, those invisible, worlds of which our outward physical universe is the mere exterior garment or body.

All these Universes are packed full with lives, some of these lives being very high, and some very low, but all are evolving, all are growing and learning entities. When any entity passes from one Universe into the next Universe on its forward evolutionary march, it enters that next Universe in the next Universe's lowest degree or world or plane or stage; and that entity thus entering we Theosophists call an Elemental in and for that Universe, because it is then in the elements of things; and it is destined to grow in that Universe which it has just entered, gaining experience, unfolding its inner powers, throwing forth what is within it as the growing tree does, and as the bud brings forth the flower — bringing out from within, as the ages pass, ever more and more of the powers locked up within itself. Thus the elemental passes from the elemental stage through all the realms of being as it rises along the Stairway of Life, passing through the human stage, becoming super-human, quasi-divine — a quasi-god,— then becoming a god. And does the Stairway end there? Is the evolutionary journey then complete? Is there an impassable barrier beyond which it cannot go? Do all things there stop in crystallized and utter perfection?

Nay! The evolving entity that we have in our mind's eye simply passes out of that Universe — the Universe into which it had previously entered and into which it has attained divinity, and passes out only to enter into a superior Universe. That other superior Universe may be entirely unseen, but it is there.

So did we humans first enter this present Universe. We, in the beginning of our evolutionary journey in our present Universe, entered this present Universe as Elementals therein, and we have grown through all the stages upwards until at present we are human beings; and we are still growing, still evolving, still pressing forwards. Do you know what evolution really is? I have often told you: Evolution is bringing out what is within, unfolding the latent powers locked up within the deathless center which every human is at the core of the core of himself. Infinitude lies there; deathlessness lies there; and therefore the pathway of growth is endless and beginningless.

The way by which to grow is to shed the personal in order to become impersonal. Do you understand? To shed, to cast aside, the limited in order to expand. How can the chick leave the egg without breaking its shell? How can the inner man expand without breaking the shell of the lower selfhood? How can the god within manifest itself — that god in each one of you, your own divine consciousness — until the imperfect, the small, the constricted, the personal in other words, has been surpassed, overpassed, left behind, abandoned, cast aside? It is in impersonality that lies immortality; in personality lies death. Therefore expand, grow, evolve, become what you are within! The gods call to us constantly — not in human words, but in those soundless symbols transmitted to us along the inner ethers which man's heart and soul interpret as spiritual instinct, aspiration, love, self-forgetfulness; and the whole import of what these voiceless messages are, is: "Come up higher!"

We humans too were Elementals once; and of course when I say 'we,' I don't mean the present evolved human being, because that would be absurd; but I mean that 'we' in far bygone periods of cosmic time were Elementals beginning our evolutionary growth in this our present Home-Universe.

Now, mark, my friends, what I shall now say to you: There is a deduction, a very important one, that I am going to ask you now to draw; and be not affrighted at it. All evolution is change; all change in evolution is growth, expansion. You cannot become something better than what you are now without leaving this present behind. Consequently, as this law applies as much to the spiritual and psychical realms as it does to the physical and astral, we draw the following deduction: There is no immortal soul in man. Do you understand? I thank the gods that it is so! Because, if there were a genuinely immortal soul in me, that soul could never grow, because it could not change; I should be forever in crystallized imperfection, because, if I changed in one atom, and by one iota, immortality would instantly vanish, because I should have become something else by the degree of that change for betterment; and evolution which is change is uninterrupted and continuous and has proceeded throughout eternity. Do you now understand the idea? This is the heart of the explanation of the teaching of the Lord Gautama the Buddha — who was the very incarnation of love and wisdom on earth because manifesting the powers of a divinity, his own inner god, his own inner Dhyâni, as we Theosophists say, the celestial entity of which he was the human expression or vehicle. And Jesus the Syrian Sage and Avatâra said exactly the same in substance when he taught: "I and my Father are one."

There are Worlds in boundless Space, there are Universes in the boundless reaches of Infinitude, in which the lowest grade of beings, the Elementals of such World or Universe, are higher in their own courses of life than those entities whom we humans call gods — and take this conception alone as an instance of the inspiring vision that Theosophy gives: so grand, so great, so wide-reaching, is the Theosophical teaching. All beings are interwoven together, all beings are interlinked together. There are only relative 'high' and 'low'; for the forces which course through us all and inspire us all and guide us all and make us all what we are, are fundamentally the same. Is it not obvious?

We change from age to age, growing always greater. Do we remain forever the same? No. We change from age to age, and this is evolutionary growth! I know not a more spirit-killing teaching in the philosophical or religious history of the globe than the teaching that man has one immortal soul which was at one time created and which thereafter is destined to endure thus for aye. This is crystallized immortality in imperfection, with no genuine growth towards a change in spiritual and cosmic values, and therefore possessing no prospect of cosmic hope! What wonder is it that men therefore ask themselves: "What is the use of trying? What is the use of trying to become something nobler than what I am?" I do not say this unkindly, my Brothers, but I stand here as a Theosophical teacher; and it is my duty to teach what I myself have been taught as best I can. "Thus have I received; thus must I pass it on."

Growth is eternal; evolution is without beginning, and it is endless. We pass through all the mansions of life, as the ages of Eternity slowly stream by into the limitless ocean of the Past. But we go steadily along, marching into an ever greater grandeur — into ever greater light. It is because of this fact that so many of the occultist and mystical societies of the world have proclaimed: "Our aim is to gain a greater light. Light, more light!"

The teaching that I have given to you is simple; anyone can understand it who thinks over it honestly. It has been taught in all ages, in all races of men, and taught by the giants in intellect possessing the deepest spiritual vision of the human race. Consult the literatures of mankind and you will see that I tell you truth. The great Visionaries have seen it; the great Teachers taught it. And all inferior men have been comforted by it.

These beings which fill universal Nature full in all their incomputable hosts have been called by different races of men by different and varying names. But you can always tell to which class or race of these beings a particular title appertains, because the attributes of such beings are usually described by the title-name. In the medieval times in European countries the 'Philosophers of Fire,' as they were called, taught about four classes of elemental beings, as respectively belonging to the element of Fire, and to the element of Air, to the element of Water, and to the element of Earth — these four elements not being the 'fire' and the 'air' and the 'water' and the 'earth' of our physical world alone; but these four names were words used technically; and the names of the inhabitants of these four so-called elements respectively were the salamanders, the sylphs, the undines, and the gnomes. Often these four classes of inhabitants were called by the generic term 'fairies.' And the instinct of humanity throughout countless ages has produced its manifold stories and legends about the fairies, so called.

I was reading the other day about a Theosophical writer, who is a Fellow, I believe, of some other Theosophical Society than ours, and who, I believe, has claimed to have photographed fairies; and these photographs were described as showing fairies clad, more or less, in medieval European costume. And I said to myself, how accommodating those fairies are! Why should they be dressed in costumes of the humans of European medieval days, unless perhaps they are described as so clad because medieval writers depict them as wearing the clothing and costumes of their own medieval periods? Why should fairies retain medieval costume? Why should they not be dressed in top hats and swallow-tail coats, or in sweaters and puttees, or again in hoop-skirts, crinolines, and bustles? Possibly five hundred years from now some other speculative writer will photograph with some etheric instrument of that future age — or think he does — pictures of entities clad as we at present are, and say: "Here! See my pictures of fairies!" It should seem obvious that one can photograph only that which can be photographed, and which the photographic plate chemically prepared can entrap as an image borne to it on the wings of material light.

Whether we call these entities nature-sprites or nature-spirits, or call them Elementals as we Theosophists do, or call them *devas* or *devatâs*, as the Hindûs do, or call them by some other name, or call them *daimonia* as the Greeks and Romans did, or speak of them as elves and kobolds, or sylphs and undines, or fairies, or what not, as medieval Europeans have done — the mere name matters not at all. Let us get the truth about them, as to what they are, where they dwell, how they came into their dwelling-places, how long they are going to stay there, when they will leave, and what their purpose in dwelling there is. All this is knowing something about them indeed.

You can get all this by proper study. An easier way is by cultivating certain faculties, which every human being has latent within him. These faculties can be cultivated. The first rule leading to success in such cultivation of faculty is given in the answer to the inevitable question: "For what art thou doing this? Is it in order to benefit mankind, in order to help the world of which you are an inseparable part, or is it for some selfish or quasi-selfish purpose of your own?"

Selfishness is an infallible bar in gaining knowledge in Occultism. You cannot join the angels, to speak in Christian terms, unless your own being has become angelic. You cannot confabulate with the gods, unless you yourself have become godlike and can breathe that sublime ether where they sit on their azure seats of power — their own spiritual selfhood. The nature-spirits, the Elementals, cannot confabulate with men until they have become like men. In order to come into touch with the Masters of Wisdom and Compassion and Peace — our Elder Brothers — you must become at least somewhat like unto them. Then all that they have is yours for the asking. Such is the law, and it is just, and it is comforting.

Be self-forgetful; be kindly; keep your heart filled with impersonal love; forgive; and then you will get the Vision, because you will have become unselfishly selfless — which means impersonal. There will then be no veils blinding you. Your mind will not be filled with the fevered thoughts of your own daily wishes for personal gain; but your mind will have expanded *pari passu* with your heart, so that heart and mind will take in and embrace others than your limited, personal, restricted self. Do you understand this? The secret lies in expansion! You must grow and expand in order to gain knowledge of what lies over the horizon! There is the secret of impersonal growth and it is the secret of gaining both knowledge and power.

Yes, these nature-spirits, or by whatever name you choose to call them, have been written about by romancers of all times; they have been written about by philosophers and religionists; their existence and their nature have been taught in the esoteric Mystery-Schools of ancient times. Some of these beings are inexpressibly beautiful; others are horrible. Some are friendly, and some are malignant to men. But all have their places in the universal scheme of things. What is poison, for instance, to human flesh, may be like the elixir of life to other entities. Poisons can cure as well as kill. Therefore judge not because some classes of these invisible entities are unfriendly to us men. They also have their place in the scheme of things, even as we humans have. They too are growing and learning entities on their upward way.

There is nothing at all so dangerous to the explorer in these invisible realms, as fear. Fear is fatal. You must be beyond fear; you must replace fear with love. He whose heart is filled with impersonal love fears never. Then you are safe. And you cannot love if your whole being is personalized, if it is constricted, if it is selfish. Love and it are opposite poles. Therefore love impersonally; and an excellent practice, in order to cultivate this sublime power, this grand occult power which can move even the hills, is to learn to forgive your fellows. If you bear even a grudge, then you poison your own life-stream. Therefore, for your own protection, hate not; for you yourself, the hater, will be the first to suffer.

I tell you, my Brothers, that ethics are based on Nature's fundamental laws. Ethics are not mere conventions. And when I speak of ethics, I don't mean any one human being's particular idea of what ethics are, but the grand moral principles of human conduct which the ages have proved and found to be grand.

Bulwer Lytton, the author of *Zanoni*, makes the wise Mejnour say to Glyndon:

Now in space there are millions of beings, not literally spiritual, for they have all, like the animalculae unseen by the naked eye, certain forms of matter, though matter so delicate. . . . Yet, in truth, these races differ most widely . . . *some of surpassing wisdom, some of horrible malignity; some hostile as fiends to men, others, gentle as messengers between earth and heaven.*"

And why should these entities not have these different and varying types of character? How about us human beings? Are all human beings perfect? Don't we humans show these same virtues and these same vices? Is it not true that some men hate and are as malignant as fiends to their brothers? Is it not true that other human beings are like gods on earth, and that to be in their presence is a blessing? Kindliness and love and wisdom radiate from them like rays from the sun.

H. P. Blavatsky, the great founder of the Theosophical Society in our own age, comments upon this extract from *Zanoni:*

> Such is the insufficient sketch of Elemental Beings void of Divine Spirit, given by one whom many with reason believed to know more than he was prepared to admit in the face of an incredulous public. We have underlined the few lines *than which nothing can be more graphically descriptive.* An Initiate, having a personal knowledge of these creatures, could do no better.

But these elemental beings are far inferior to man. Man stands midway along the Stairway of Life, or the pathway of evolving entities, between the gods on the one hand, and these beings beneath him on the other hand. And yet, could we (which is impossible — but could we) eliminate them from the Universe, take them out from the Universe, then the Universe would fall to pieces, and crumble into impalpable cosmic dust, because these minor beings, these growing entities below man, are the elemental spirits of Nature, what we Theosophists call the Elementals, and in very truth they form the material fabric and structure of the Universe. They surround us always: we pass without knowing it through the various grades of ether and substance in which they live and dwell and have their being; we breathe them in and exhale them again; they are in our flesh, in the air we breathe, they are in the water, in the earth, in the plants, in the spaces; they are everywhere; and they are with human beings and with the gods, the grand cosmic Workers; they have their places in the Cosmic Work just as men have and just as the gods have. They all help to the same Cosmic Ends; and that is why they are here. They have their inevitable places, and they are growing and evolving entities just as we humans are growing and evolving entities; they will grow and evolve and finally become men; but then we humans shall have grown to become gods.

Forget it not: we once in far bygone aeons were just such nature-sprites or Elementals. But even then — just as it is at present — locked up within each one of us then existing as an elemental being, there was the inner god, unable to express itself as yet because the vehicle was so imperfect, even as the vehicle now in us human beings is too imperfect for a full manifestation of the splendor of the inner divinity; but nevertheless the inner god was always there as the spiritual point, the vital and central point of consciousness; and let us not forget also that these gods themselves are growing, changing, advancing, evolving.

There is no death; there is no death anywhere; there is but composition and dissolution; and it is between these two continuously interchanging states of endless life that we learn; it is by means of these two processes that we grow. It is thus that the child becomes the man, changing, passing, from childhood to manhood: the child was, and then is not, but the man succeeds him. No entity anywhere at any time remains changeless, for this would be an immortality in crystallized imperfection, and the idea is both horrible and repulsive because it is flagrantly untrue.

Yes, the Elementals are everywhere about us. The blood which flows in my body is driven by their power, guided, however, by my automatic mental action — the vegetative part of my mental constitution. I am born of the Elementals; they have born me this body; and I have been the grand architect of this body of mine through my overshadowing soul; and these elemental workers have followed the impress which my vitality has given to them and have builded for me the temple, the physical temple of flesh, in which I live. To them I am a god, just as to us human beings the gods seem so grand. And yet in the realms of the divine, the gods who inhabit these realms are but imperfect entities compared with other superior spheres inhabited by entities still more sublime.

The Elementals are growing beings, learning entities, evolving elemental souls, passing through phase after phase of existence in innumerable imbodiments succeeding each other throughout countless time. I pray you understand this idea. It is as simple as it is grand, and it is a wonderful key; it is a key to many great mysteries.

I have some questions here, which I have been requested to answer. I will do so briefly.

> There is a school of Theosophists developing a Western Occultism. I have noticed that you never mention Western Occultism but seem to confine yourself exclusively to Tibetan or Hindû Occultism. Why should not the West develop a system of Occultism of its own, a union of Eastern esotericism with the proved discoveries of modern science? This, I believe, is the object of the school I refer to. Why should it not be supported as a progressive step in Theosophy?

Why not? But nevertheless the statement as regards myself is not true. Often have I spoken of the great Occultists of the West. But it is an absurdity to suppose that there can be an Eastern Occultism, and a Western Occultism, and a Northern Occultism, and a Southern Occultism. Occultism is simply the science of the things which are hid. You cannot have an Eastern chemistry, and a Western chemistry, and a Northern chemistry, and a Southern chemistry. Chemistry is chemistry, however much schools which teach chemistry may differ from each other It is an absurdity to talk about the 'Occultism of the West' except in so far as the literatures treat the fundamental subject differently from the manner in which Orientals have treated the 'Occultism of the East.' Occultism is the science of the things that are hid, that are unseen; and no true Occultist exists except he who has been initiated. Mystics exist — many of them — without having passed through the initiatory rites; and there have been many grand Mystics; mysticisms of many kinds exist, according to the temperament of the writer or the thinker or the feeler. But there is but one Occultism — the science of things unseen.

Therefore teaching the Occultism of any people, whether of the East or of the West, whether of the North or of the South, is teaching universal Occultism; and merely to consult the literatures of Oriental writers on Occultism or Western writers on Occultism is merely an exercise in literary instruction, and that exercise is a good thing to follow; but nevertheless there are not two or three or more kinds of Occultism. There cannot be. If so, then genuine Occultism would be untrue. It is the science and elucidation of the things which are hid, unseen, and which comprise, as I have told you on other occasions from this platform, the structure and operations of the Universe in which we and all the hosts of entities visible and invisible live and move and have our being; and this explanation means especially of the invisible Universe — the illimitable ranges along the endless Stairway of Life which obviously our imperfect physical eyes cannot see, and which our imperfectly developed brain-mind finds it so difficult to understand.

So far as a union of Eastern esotericism with the proved discoveries of modern science is concerned, I lectured from this platform some few years ago, for some six months or more, on that very subject; and these lectures have been printed in a book* which anyone of you can read.

The next question that I have been asked to answer this afternoon is the following:

I consider myself practically a Theosophist —

He has a good opinion of himself. I *try* to be a Theosophist.

— although as yet I have joined no Theosophical Society. I admire the loftiness of the thought in your lectures, but notice that you stress mostly selflessness and do not give much attention to branches of Occultism that

---

Theosophy and Modern Science, 2 volumes, $5.00: Theosophical University Press, Point Loma, California.

interest many Theosophists. In another Theosophical Society they also claim to teach selflessness but in addition give interesting information regarding occult powers. Do you not think that more people would join your Society if you would do the same?

It is quite possible that we should gain members more quickly, but I am inclined to think that I don't want that kind of inquirers to predominate in our membership. The Theosophical Society is constantly teaching the Wisdom of the Gods; and I call upon every genuine heart and thinking mind to join with us in our sublime work. Come then, and help us! I can show you the way leading to your own inner god; but if any one of you comes thinking that you are going to gain powers for yourself merely in order 'to put it over' on your fellows, then I pray to you to keep out. Cleanse your hearts, my Brothers; then when this is done, come, and both my hands will be ready to take yours. 'A clean mind, a pure heart, an unveiled spiritual perception'— even the beginning of these three sublime virtues will entitle you to all the wisdom of the gods, given to you progressively as you grow.

So far as Occultism goes, I have talked about that sublime subject on many, many different occasions. I teach it. Teaching is part of my Theosophical duty; but the more secret things of Occultism that I teach are kept well secret. I will tell you this: Self-advertisement for the mere end of gaining adherents puts those who thus advertise their wares — where? The man, the organization, the society, which has something valuable to give is soon discovered by those who are hungry for the truth that can be found there. Inquirers soon discover it. They discover where it is; and thither they go. Any human being believing in the only prerequisite to fellowship in The Theosophical Society, which sole prerequisite is an honest belief in Universal Brotherhood, is cordially invited to join us.

We Theosophists have no dogmas. You don't have to believe any thing on blind faith. I tell you that fact on every Sunday when I speak to you, and if anything I say to you at any time seems to you to be wrong, reject it — and thus be an honest man. In doing so you are at least exercising your powers of spiritual judgment; and even though you make a mistake, as it is probable that you will, nevertheless in continuing that spiritual exercise you will grow spiritually. We in The Theosophical Society are not teachers of blind faith.

Some Theosophists say that we should develop our powers and become Adepts, while others say we should simply be unselfish and work for humanity and that the powers will come of themselves. If we develop our powers and thereby come closer to the great Masters, will not unselfishness follow as a logical sequence?

No! The mere developing of powers is easy, very easy; and it is precisely the thing that the *chela,* the disciple, the pupil, is taught *not* to do — taught not to try to develop powers when he takes his first steps on the path of Occultism. The magicians of the African deserts, the Voodoo-doctors, the savages and barbarians of the earth, can easily teach you, for instance, how to hypnotise. This is not at all difficult to do. But why do you want to learn hypnotism? To gain for yourself some selfish advantage or to satisfy the selfish craving for power. Do you think that any true spiritual teacher would teach such things as that? The Teacher's duty is to bring light, peace, help, consolation, to broken hearts and to souls afire with the hunger for truth. As regards powers, these will come in good time, and they will be the spiritual powers; and the spiritual powers are the grandest and most potent of all, and they will come only when you shall have learned to use them wisely and unselfishly. They cannot be used otherwise.

No, you cannot approach the *âśrama,* the seat of the Masters of Wisdom and Compassion and Peace, merely by developing your powers. The only way to reach them is, as I have told you before, by becoming like unto them. Will ye reach the gods? Then become godlike. If ye wish to be disciples of the great Masters of Wisdom and Peace, then become like unto them; and if the wish to do this is in your heart, you will be shown the way. The Masters are waiting and ready; but they accept as disciples only those who can understand what they teach (is it not obvious?), and who can bear the burden of the responsibilities which accompany conferred knowledge and developed powers. Powers then will come to you — spiritual powers, intellectual powers, psychical powers, even physical powers; but no spiritual teacher will ever teach you how to develop your powers, except on spiritual and moral and intellectual grounds and after long and arduous tests safely passed through; because unless you are ready, spiritually and intellectually prepared, he would be putting an engine of destruction into your hands, and you, the receiver, would be the first victim of the fatal gift.

Men in general do not arm lunatics — who, alas! are among us — and send them out to wreak havoc in the world. We do not put poisons and explosives in the hands of little children and then send them forth to play. Such likewise is the principle of prudence and wisdom which lies in the laws of occult training. But be like unto the Masters, my Brothers, and you will find them; because in very fact they will come to you. And then in time your powers will develop as easily and naturally as the flower grows. This is a promise; it is a statement of exact and literal truth. Too often has it been supposed that putting power into unprepared hands is the way by which to reach the gods. The idea is all wrong. No human being can gain spiritual powers until he has proved that he is prepared to use them aright; and if any human being has a contrary idea it is because he is either thoughtless or evil-minded.

The following is a question, friends, which I was very doubtful about answering. I will read it:

I was formerly a member of the Theosophical Society of which Annie Besant is the head, but now am a follower of our revered Teacher, J. Krishnamurti, who has shown us the true path to enlightenment. Many of my former comrades are criticizing our Teacher, J. Krishnamurti, as having departed from Theosophy. As I suppose you have no prejudices in this matter, I wish to ask your opinion as to whether it is reasonable to do this, seeing that the two leaders of Mrs. Besant's society — Mrs. Besant herself and Bishop Leadbeater — endorsed our Teacher, J. Krishnamurti, as the incarnation of a World-Soul, and they themselves accepted him as their Teacher? If they have changed their minds, do we have to do the same? Should we not follow the World-Teacher in preference? So far as I know, although both are of course very advanced Theosophists, they do not claim to be World-Teachers.

I answer this question with extreme reluctance. It is not really my business to deal with the internal affairs of some other Theosophical Society; and furthermore, Mrs. Besant, Mr. Leadbeater, and Mr. Krishnamurti, are not members of ours and have naught to do with us. They are leading spirits in another Theosophical Society, and I have no doubt that all three are trying to do their best, and I suppose that they do what they think is right; and had I known from whom this question came, I should have returned the question and have suggested that the matter be placed before Mrs. Besant or Mr. Leadbeater or Mr. Krishnamurti.

Of course it seems that the querent, the questioner, thinks that Mr. Krishnamurti is a 'World-Teacher.' I do not think that he is. I think that Mr. Krishnamurti is a well-meaning, kindly-hearted young man. I see no signs at all of his being a World-Teacher or any other sign that would induce me to think that he is approaching that sublime state. I see in him and in his teachings neither the profound wisdom, nor the intellectual penetration, nor — and this perhaps is the real test — the esoteric knowledge. But this of course is *my* opinion. I have no doubt that Mr. Krishnamurti is a most excellent young man trying to do what he thinks is right; and if any have found help in following his teachings — simple, and, in a way, only a moderately successful rehash of some of the teachings of the Hindû Upanishads — then I am glad of it for their sakes; and I wish Mr. Krishnamurti well as long as he continues in his efforts to help others.

As regards Mrs. Besant's and Mr. Leadbeater's former and present opinion of their protégé, I have naught to say. That is their affair alone and it is for them to give any answer that they may please to this question. It is not my business. I could, of course, tell you what I think; but what good would that be to you? However, perhaps as the question has been asked of me, as a Theosophical Teacher it is my duty to make a few further comments, and therefore I will go a little farther and say: My heart has ached because of the troubled situation of brother-Theosophists in that Society. I would give anything if I could bring help to them. I have already extended my right hand in genuine fellowship, and it is still outstretched. I have received heartfelt responses from many individuals, although not from all; and I am encouraged.

But the troubles of these other Theosophists in their own Society are their own affair, and they must find a way out for themselves. If I can give any help at any time, and in any way, I shall be heart-happy to do so. I cannot do more than that. They have brought forth teachings other than the original teachings of the founders of the Theosophical Society, and if those who accept these new teachings find them good, and are satisfied, then I have naught to say to them on that score. But how can I bring help to a man who won't accept it? I feel that I cannot answer at greater length this question as to whether members of Mrs. Besant's Society should follow her or should follow Mr. Krishnamurti, her one-time protégé. That is a question which I feel it would be improper for me even to try to answer.

My Brothers, before closing I want to tell you something that I bring to your attention on every Sunday afternoon when we meet here together: it is a recalling to your mind and to your heart of your divine ancestry. You as human beings sit before me as human beings; but looking beyond and behind the veil of flesh, I can see the sublime lineaments of a god in each one of you. I can sense the divinity sleeping in the heart of your heart; and I feel, as I stand here and speak to you, that I am addressing an audience of the gods as it were in highest Olympus, seated on their azure seats of power, these azure seats being for each one of them his own divine selfhood. Men, you are gods feebly expressing through your imperfect human vehicle, through your imperfectly evolved humanity, the divine powers and faculties in you.

Oh! if I could implant this seed of thought and feeling in your hearts and minds, so that it would take root and grow there and thus change your lives, I should feel that I, a man, had done a god's work — the work of a god! But the god within me appeals to the god within you, and urges me to tell you: Man, know thyself, thy inner divine Self, for it is one with Boundless Infinitude, of which you are, each one of you, an inseparable part.

This is the end of this publication.

Any remaining blank pages are for our book binding
requirements and are blank on purpose.

To search thousands of interesting publications like this one,
please remember to visit our website at:

Printed in the United States
52436LVS00004B/1